**Aboriginal Global Pioneers
Book 4**

Australian Aboriginal Fire

Managing Country

Marji Hill

Published by The Prison Tree Press 2024
Copyright © 2024 Marji Hill

The Prison Tree Press
Suite 124
1-10 Albert Avenue
Broadbeach, Queensland 4218
https://marjihill.com
https://www.fastselfpublishing.com

Disclaimer:
All the material contained in this book is provided for educational and informational purposes only. No responsibility can be taken for any results or outcomes resulting from the use of this material.

While every care has been taken to trace and acknowledge copyright the publishers tender their apologies for any accidental infringement where copyright has proved untraceable.

Every attempt has been made to provide information that is both accurate and effective, however, the author does not assume any responsibility for the accuracy or use/misuse of this information.

Acknowledgement is given to Canva for most of the illustrations in this book.

A catalogue record for this work is available from the National Library of Australia

Aboriginal Global Pioneers (Series of 5 Books)

ISBN 978-0-9756571-8-8 Hardback
ISBN 978-0-9756571-9-5 eBook

Australian Non-Fiction | First Nations | History

Acknowledgements

I acknowledge the Traditional Custodians of Country
throughout Australia
and their connections to land, sea, and community.

I pay my respect to elders, past, present, and emerging
and extend my respect to all First Nations peoples today.

In the spirit of reconciliation,
my mission is to increase understanding
between the First Nations and other Australians
and to provide people from all over the globe
some basic understanding of Australia's first people,
their history, and cultures.

Marji Hill

Contents

INTRODUCTION

On New Year's Day 2020, Australia was on fire. Massive, uncontrollable bushfires swept across the country.

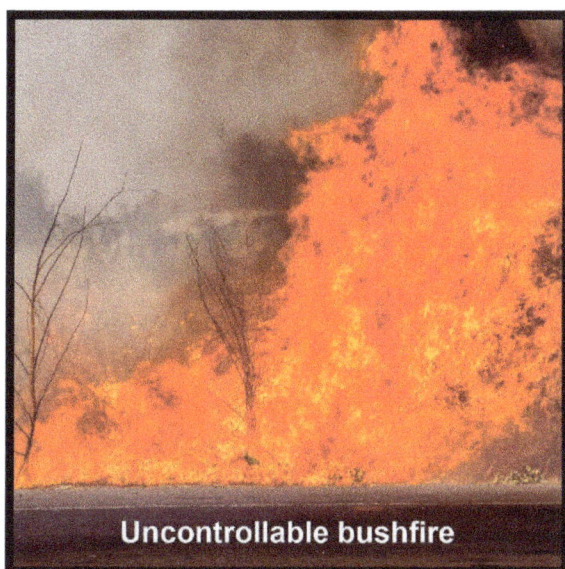

Uncontrollable bushfire

The continent was burning. This was unprecedented; it was apocalyptic.

These catastrophic fires put Australia into a state of national crisis and emergency.

The continent experienced:

      mass regional evacuations;
      shocking heat waves;
      choking smoke;
      eerie atmosphere;

devastating loss of life, property, wildlife, stock and livelihood.

Millions of native animals were destroyed.

Millions of native animals were destroyed

Thousands of people trapped by fires were rescued.

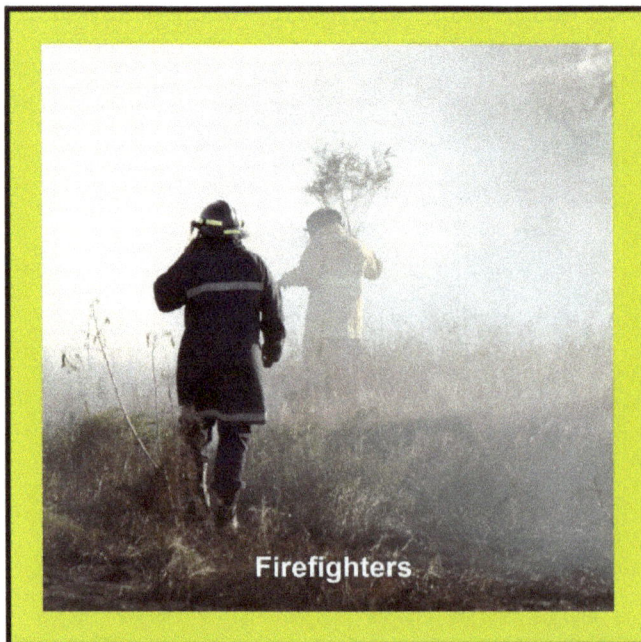

Thousands were rescued

SIGNIFICANCE OF FIRE

For most Australians fire is always a threat, a destructive force. For thousands and thousands of years, experience has taught us how to control fire and put it to use.

But that is not the whole narrative.

For Australia's First Nations people, fire holds great spiritual meaning with stories, memories and dance being passed down around the variety of roles that fire plays.

It has been used as a tool going back as far as 65,000 years ago and possibly even longer.

Fire has been used in hunting, cooking, for warmth and for managing country.

Not only does fire connect First Nations people to Country, it has great symbolic significance in First Nations customs.

It is something that can be controlled and it has been a fundamental element of traditional First Nations cultures for many centuries.

First Nations people have been so successful at controlling fire they drastically reshaped the Australian environment over thousands of years.

First Nations people
reshaped the Australian environment

Converted over thousands of years

LAND MANAGEMENT

Fire was deliberately used for land management in First Nations cultures.

Early European observers noted a mosaic pattern of deliberate burning which was done frequently.

First Nations people burned great tracks of land across the continent every winter. Captain James Cook and Sir Joseph Banks recorded seeing smoke from large fires as they sailed up the east coast of Australia.

The Dutch navigators as they travelled up the west coast of Australia noted large fires. There were controlled burns of dry grasslands or forests that were cluttered with debris.

In 1791 George Vancouver, the English navigator, described a small river near King George Sound in Western Australia that bordered extensive plains and meadows.

The nature of the countryside made it easy for his party to travel inland. He noted how the stems of gumtrees had been scorched.

The open grassy plains were the result of thousands of years of controlled burning by First Nations people. This is something not realised by the early European observers.

Neither they did know that the forests of straight-stemmed trees had been cleared of undergrowth by selective burning over thousands of years.

CLEARING THE LAND

First Nations people used fire to clear the land. They did this to control weeds and for clearing undergrowth by removing dead branches and long grass. This was to reduce danger from uncontrolled bushfires.

It was also a method for coaxing wildlife to come and graze on the fresh grass.

This in turn made it easier to hunt for food. While the animals were eating, First Nations hunters could more easily catch and kill their prey.

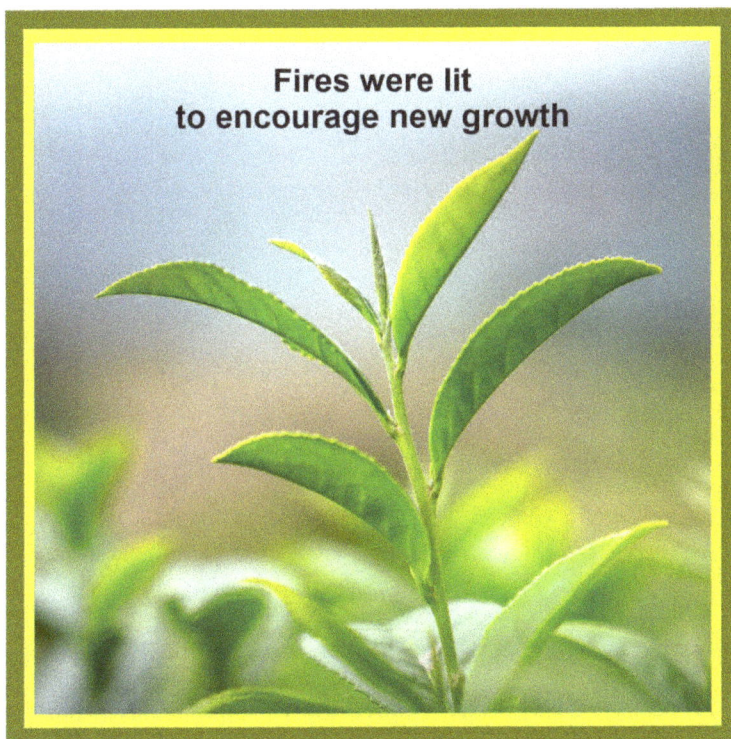

Fires were lit to encourage new growth

Fire was also used to drive animals into the open when they were hunting.

Fires were lit to encourage new growth as some native plants will only release their seeds after they have been burned. Controlled burns stimulated the regeneration of fresh grass and saplings.

Overall fire was used to increase the productivity of the environment. It helped the regrowth of plants and ensured a plentiful supply of food.

Country was systematically burned on a rotating mosaic pattern.

The timing of burn-offs was always important. For example, the timing for burning stringybark in Awu-Laya country in far north Queensland is after the emus have finished their breeding. Emus nest in the stringybark country because it is greener and safer.

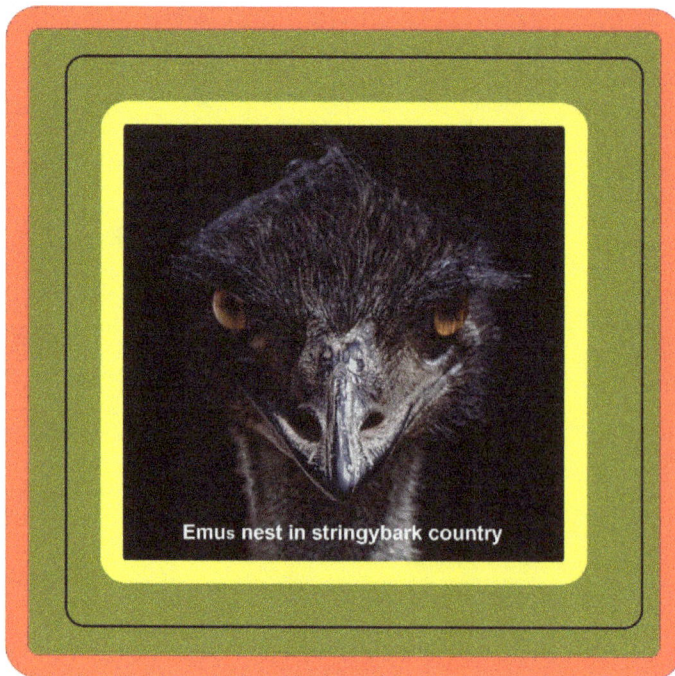

Emus nest in stringybark country

Weather conditions had to be taken into account and neighbouring groups had to be notified about an impending burn. Burn-offs had to be avoided when the growing season was on.

Using fire to manage country meant First Nations people were able to open up new areas of land to live in. It was difficult to travel through dense bushland and heavily timbered forests. It was also difficult to find food.

By persistent burning of the country, fire-sensitive bush trees in the forests were replaced by fire-resistant eucalypts and scrub. In turn these were replaced by heath and scrub which shelter a variety of animals and birds and provide a range of edible plants and roots.

Thus, uninhabitable forests were transformed into land in which people could live.

**Uninhabitable forests were transformed
into land in which people could live**

Fire was not only used just to get rid of unwanted plants and trees.

The Anbara people of north-central Arnhem Land in the Northern Territory used fire to maintain rather than destroy the existing vegetation. Every three or four years the Anbara people burned every part of their grasslands, open scrub and eucalyptus woodland.

These fires were low in intensity because the dead leaves and branches had never been allowed to build up excessively.

Some plants do not regenerate well after burning. The Anbara people did not burn areas of thick forest because of the edible plants they sheltered which fire would destroy.

In order to protect these plants, they attached religious taboos to them. Anyone breaking these taboos was in danger of experiencing the wrath of angry Ancestral beings who dwelt in those patches of forest.

Wide fire-breaks were burned around these forests soon after the wet season finished so they could not accidentally burn. These precious plants remained unharmed during the dry season when burning was carried out between June and August.

A CHANGED LANDSCAPE

These regular burn-offs changed the landscape in various ways. Heavy forested areas were opened up so that people could travel through them with ease. Extensive grassy areas were created so animals could graze.

The growth of fire-resistant plants was encouraged because they survived burn-offs and did not compete with other kinds of plants.

MAKING FIRE

The first step in learning how to control fire was to learn how to make it. Once this had been achieved, First Nations people carried smouldering branches about with them so that they could light fire wherever they went.

But there were times when there was nowhere to get fire from or anybody with whom to share a fire. People then needed to know how to make it themselves.

Making fire

Fire can be made by friction. It takes a skilled person at least five minutes to get a spark by twirling a pointed hard-wood stick in a soft-wood stick. When the two dry wooden surfaces were rubbed together at high speed, it was possible to produce enough heat to cause a flame.

Another friction technique was to make a shallow hole in a piece of wood and then fill it with a mix of crushed leaves and dry grass. The sharpened end of another piece of wood was then pushed down into the hole and spun quickly backwards and forwards.

The friction eventually generated sufficient heat to smoulder the grass and blown on until it burst into flame.

Fire was also made by striking together two hard rock surfaces such as basalt, and thus producing a spark.

FIRE IN SOCIAL LIFE

In outback communities, fires are lit in the backyards of homes or near where people have set up camps. These campfires serve several purposes.

Campfire

They are the pivotal points for social gatherings. Men and women sit around the fire to talk, to play cards, or to plan ceremonies.

Today as in the past, people work beside their fires. They make paintings, carvings, boomerangs and woomeras. They make ornate barbed spear blades, digging sticks, and straighten new spear shafts. They weave baskets. Fire was used to boil and dye grasses that are woven into bags and baskets.

They repaired tools, talked, taught children, or prepared food for a meal.

Fire is a tool that people use. When people are sitting and working around their fires, the fire is not just to provide warmth.

Fire is a part of life.

COOKING

Cooking

Fire, of course, was essential for preparing some foods. Apart from using simple techniques for cooking meat over coals, they also used other techniques. For example, they broiled fish over open coals or wrapped them in large leaves before steaming them.

Sometimes they dug pits and built fires in them. When the fires burned down an emu or wallaby was placed over the glowing coals, covered with branches and dirt, and then let to roast in its own juices.

FIRE IN CEREMONIES

Fire had its place in rituals, songs and stories.

First Nations people still use their ancient skills for the preparation of ritual objects which they use in ceremonies. The preparation of these, particularly those fashioned from wood, is a preliminary part of religious ceremonies.

It was believed that fire could drive away evil spirits. Anyone who left their campfire at night carried a burning fire-stick . If they heard any strange noises they would throw their fire-stick into the darkness to frighten off any evil spirits who were hovering around.

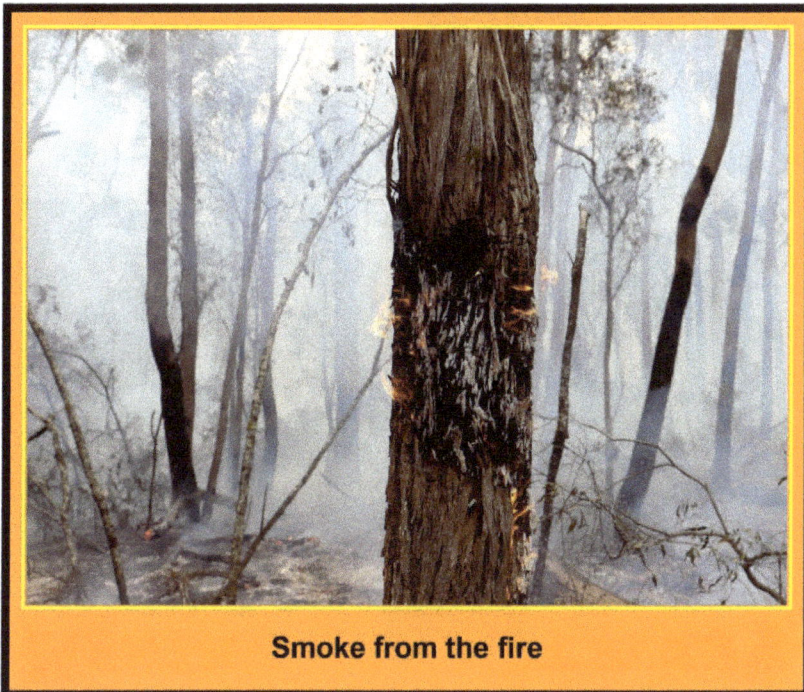

Smoke from the fire

First Nations people believed that fire encouraged the spirits of the dead to return to their own spirit centre. They burned the dwellings of people who had recently died together with all their personal belongings.

Fire was used in funeral rituals to encourage the spirits of the dead to leave the place where they had lived and return to their spirit centre from which they had been born.

Smoke from the fire was used to ritually cleanse people before and after ceremonies.

In ceremonies, fire provided the smoke to purify those taking part and to drive away spirits of the dead.

A smoking ceremony, which involves smouldering various native plants to produce smoke, has cleansing properties and can ward off bad spirits. It can be used for healing, spiritual renewal and in funeral rites.

Smoking Ceremony

These days, given that Australia is prone to catastrophic bushfires, there is a shift in national consciousness about land management and bush fire prevention.

First Nations senior people, distressed about what happens to people and the land in these massive wildfires, say that people are not looking after Country. They talk about Country in the same way they would talk about a person.

They talk to their Country, sing to it, visit it and worry about it.

People are not looking after Country

They say we have to care for Country. This is necessary for the health of the land.

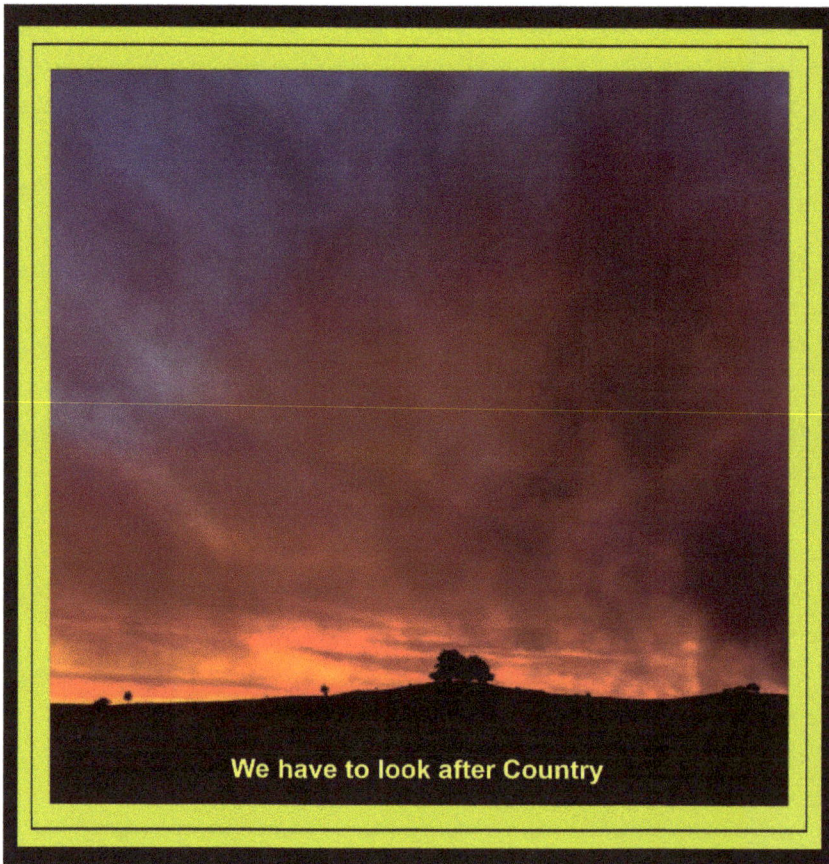

We have to look after Country

Many First Nations people feel that if Country is wild or sick it is not being managed properly by those responsible for it. They say we have to look after it. The relationship is reciprocal because if you look after Country it will look after you.

Australians can well learn fire management practices from First Nations peoples and integrate it into the national bushfire response.

Glossary

Apocalyptic Describing the complete destruction of the world

Catastrophic Involving or causing sudden great damage or suffering

Evacuations The act of moving people from a dangerous place to somewhere safe

Reciprocal Something done in return

Woomeras A First Nations implement used to throw a spear more forcibly

Sources

The author acknowledges the following sources of information.

Barlow, Alex *Fire.* 1994 South Melbourne, Vic, Macmillan. (Aboriginal Technology)

Flanagan, Richard 2020 "Australia is committing climate suicide" *New York Times*. January 3.

Gillies, Christopher 2017 "Traditional Aboriginal burning in modern day land management " https://landcareaustralia.org.au/project/traditional-aboriginal-burning-modern-day-land-management/

Pascoe, Bruce 2019 *Young Dark Emu: A Truer History* Broome, Magabala.

Rose, D 1996 in https://aiatsis.gov.au/sites/default/files/research_pub/benefits-cfc_0_2.pdf 7

Steffensen, Victor 2020 *Fire Country: How Indigenous Fire Management Could Help Save Australia*. Richmond, Vic., Harley Grant Travel.

Who is Marji Hill

Marji Hill, artist and painter since childhood, runs her art career alongside her career as an author.

She is a highly respected international author as well as a seasoned business executive, researcher and coach.

Marji is passionate about promoting understanding between Australia's first people and other Australians.

The spirit of reconciliation was fostered in all her writings ever since she was a Research Fellow in Education at the Australian Institute of Aboriginal and Torres Strait Islander Studies (AIATSIS) in Canberra.

From 2008 to 2011, Marji was Deputy Chairperson of the Mosman Branch of Reconciliation Australia in Sydney.

Following her Research Fellowship at AIATSIS in 1976 Marji, together with her late partner, Alex Barlow, produced more than seventy (70) books on all aspects of the First Nations people including the critical, annotated bibliography *Black Australia*.

In 1989 she was the Project Coordinator and one of the researchers and writers of *Australian Aboriginal Culture* the official Australian Government publication on First Nations people.

In 1988 *Six Australian Battlefields* was published by Angus and Robertson. A decade later it was re-published by Allen & Unwin as a paperback edition.

Her nine-volume encyclopaedia, *Macmillan Encyclopaedia of Australia's Aboriginal Peoples* was published in 2000 and in 2009 she published *The Apology: Saying Sorry To The Stolen Generations*.

Marji's more recent publications extend to self-improvement and self-help with books like *Staying Young Growing Old* and *Inspired by Country* a self-help book about painting with gouache.

More Books by Marji Hill

First Nations

Hill, Marji 2021 *Australian Aboriginal History: 5 Stories of Indigenous Heroes.* Broadbeach, Qld, The Prison Tree Press.

Hill, Marji 2021 *First People Then and Now: Introducing Indigenous Australians.* 2nd ed. Broadbeach, Qld, The Prison Tree Press.

Aboriginal Global Pioneers

Hill, Marji 2024 *Australian Aboriginal Origins: Earliest Beginnings.* Broadbeach, Qld, The Prison Tree Press. (Book 1)

Hill, Marji 2024 *Australian Aboriginal Trade: Sharing Goods and Services.* Broadbeach, Qld, The Prison Tree Press. (Book 2)

Hill, Marji 2024 *Australian Aboriginal Religion: Country and Dreaming.* Broadbeach, Qld, The Prison Tree Press. (Book 3)

Hill, Marji 2024 *Australian Aboriginal Fire: Managing Country.* Broadbeach, Qld, The Prison Tree Press. (Book 4)

Hill, Marji 2024 *Australian Aboriginal Medicine: Caring for People.* Broadbeach, Qld, The Prison Tree Press. (Book 5)

Self-improvement/Self-Help

Hill, Marji 2014 *Staying Young Growing Old.* Broadbeach, Qld, The Prison Tree Press.

Hill, Marji 2020 *How Big Is Your Why? An Author's Guide to Time Management and Productivity to Achieve Transformational Results.* Broadbeach, Qld, The Prison Tree Press.

Hill, Marji 2020 *A Create and Publish Toolbox: 101 Prompts In A Guided Journal To Help You Write, Self-publish, And Market Your Book On Amazon.* Broadbeach, Qld, The Prison Tree Press.

Hill, Marji 2021 *Inspired by Country: An Artist's Journey Back to Nature, Landscape Painting with Gouache.* Broadbeach, Qld, The Prison Tree Press.

Hill, Marji 2024 *Australian Paintings: Artworks by Marji Hill.* Broadbeach, Qld, The Prison Tree Press.

Gold

Hill, Marji 2022 *Gates of Gold: The Discovery of Gold, its Legacy and its Contribution to Australian Identity* Broadbeach, Qld, The Prison Tree Press.

Hill, Marji 2022 *Shadows of Gold: Eureka and the Birth of Australian Democracy.* Broadbeach, Qld, The Prison Tree Press.

Hill, Marji 2022 *Gold and the Chinese: Racism, Riots and Protest on the Australian Goldfields.* Broadbeach, Qld, The Prison Tree Press.

Hill, Marji 2022 *Ghosts of Gold: The Life and Times of Jupiter Mosman.* Broadbeach, Qld, The Prison Tree Press.

Hill, Marji 2022 *Blood Gold: Native Police, Bushrangers & Law and Order on the Goldfields.* Broadbeach, Qld, The Prison Tree Press.

www.ingramcontent.com/pod-product-compliance
Lightning Source LLC
Chambersburg PA
CBHW040254100426
42811CB00011B/1260